YOU ARE WORTH MORE

ULTIMATE GUIDE TO SELF CARE AND RESPECT

YOU ARE WORTH MORE

Wisdom T.T

Acknowledgement

I greatly thank and acknowledge God for the strength and ideas in putting this wonderful piece together. I thank my supporters, family and friends for immense support. Lastly I commend myself on being willful, determined and deliberate till the end of the production.

Table of Contents.

Introduction

The world is full of people who don't take care of themselves and don't show much respect for their bodies. As a result, they suffer from mental and physical illness that could have been prevented in the first place. But what if you weren't one of those people? What would happen if you learned how to love yourself? That's exactly what I'm going to do with this book! It took me years before I realized how important self-love is but now that it's dawned on me, I decided to put it into writing.

Self-care is a very important part of being a well-rounded person. It isn't just about taking care of your body and mind, but also about taking care of your spirit as well. Taking care of yourself can help you feel better about yourself, which in turn will make you happier overall!

Self Love and Care

Self-care is defined as the personal care necessary to keep oneself healthy and strong. It is the practice of maintaining physical, mental, emotional and spiritual health stability in order to cope with life's challenges. Self-care activities can be anything from getting enough sleep a few nights in a row to brushing teeth twice a day. It can also include spending time with family and friends, joining an activity that interests you or taking up a hobby, exercising regularly or meditating more often. This definition of self-care comes from the United States Department of Health and Human Services. Respect is defined as the wants of an individual to be recognized, acknowledged especially as worthy and valuable.

Self care and self love are two important concepts that are often overlooked in our busy lives. Self care is the practice of taking time to nurture yourself and your wellbeing, while self love is the practice of showing yourself compassion, respect, and kindness. Both are essential for leading a healthy and balanced life.

Self care can take many forms, from physical activities such as exercise or yoga to mental activities such as journaling or meditation. Self love involves recognizing your own worth and treating yourself with kindness and understanding. It also involves setting boundaries with others so that you can protect your emotional wellbeing.

By practicing self care and self love, we can create a healthier relationship with ourselves which will ultimately lead to better relationships with others, and be more present with our body, emotions, thoughts, and actions.

Self Compassion

Self-compassion is a way of being with yourself that helps you overcome adversity. It's not about self-pity, self-indulgence or any other kind of negative emotion. Self-compassion is also not about indulging in your own suffering (i.e., self-denigration), but rather it involves accepting your feelings and thoughts as they are without judging yourself for them—or worse yet, feeling ashamed for having them at all!

Self compassion means being kinder to yourself than you would be if no one else had ever told you how great or good looking or smart etcetera they thought you were…it means recognizing that everyone has flaws like everyone else does…and then accepting those flaws without judgment or shame instead of trying to change something about yourself so that they don't exist anymore (which rarely works anyway).

The first step to showing compassion and love to yourself is acknowledging that you need it. The second step is understanding why you're feeling the way you do. Understanding why can be complicated, but think about where these feelings are coming from and what has brought them on. The third step is doing something positive for yourself that makes you feel better- like going for a walk or cleaning your house. The fourth step is continuing with the tasks in order to help ease any negative emotions- this can include talking things out with someone who's supportive, focusing on something else that makes you comfortable and delighted.

Finding a Self Care Routine that Works for You

You may not be able to change the world, but you can change how you feel.

You can do it by creating a self care and self love routine that works for you in respect to your work, gender, age, circumstances.

If you want to improve your energy, if you want to feel calm and relaxed, if you want to have more focus and concentration at work, then take some time out of your day to make yourself feel good.

Here are some tips on how to create a self care and self love routine that works for you:

1.   Decide what kind of self care routine works best for you.

2.   Write down all the things that make you happy in life (this could be hobbies, relationships etc).

3.   Make a list of all the activities that make you happy (this could be exercise or meditation or getting lost in a book).

4.   Find ways to include these activities into your daily routine so that they become part of your life forever (exercise could be 30 minutes per day; meditation could be 5 minutes per day).

Self-care is the practice of taking good care of yourself. It's about learning to treat yourself well and providing for your physical, mental, emotional and spiritual needs. Self-care can be a big part of any person's self-development, especially if you're focusing on building a better relationship with yourself.

It's also important to take care of yourself because it helps you learn how to take care of others. It's better to be kind and loving with yourself than in a rush to get through your day without giving yourself some time to relax and breathe.

Whether you have an existing routine or not, creating a self-care routine is an important first step toward self development. Here are some tips on how to create a self care routine that works for you:

The first step to creating a self care and self love routine that works for you is identifying what your needs are.

Do you need more time to yourself? Are you struggling with anxiety or depression? Do you feel like you're not good enough? If so, it's important to take the time to reflect and assess the situation.

Creating a self care and self love routine can help us all get better at coping with stress in our lives. It can also help us feel better about ourselves and how we're doing.

Self-care and self-love are important to your overall health and well being.

Self-care is a way of taking care of yourself, so that you can better take care of others. It's about making sure you have enough energy, time and resources to do the things you want to do, so that you can be a better partner, parent or friend. It's about taking good care of your body so you can get more done in life. Self-care is also about taking good care of yourself in times when you feel overwhelmed or overworked.

The first thing to remember is that your daily routine has to be realistic. It's important to keep in mind that you don't always have to do things at the exact same time every day.

For example, if you have a morning meeting or workout in the morning, it doesn't mean you can't take a break in the afternoon for some social media time or a quick walk outside. Your daily routine should reflect your personal needs and time constraints.

Your self-care routine should look different depending on who you are, where you live and what kind of life you lead. For example:

If you live alone in an apartment then having a routine where I wake up early in the morning and spend time with my cat would be part of my self-care routine for the day. I would make sure that I ate breakfast before going into work (which takes me 45 minutes) and then take a shower before getting dressed for work. After work I would go home again because I don't have anyone else at home with me, so there isn't anyone else who needs me to take care of them either!

Maintaining Daily Routine and Practicing Self Respect

I think that everyone has a daily routine. Maybe it's something simple, like going to the gym and working out. Or maybe you have a full-time job and your daily routine involves getting up and going to the office, or maybe you're a stay at home mom and your daily routine involves spending time with family and doing things around the house.

The important thing is that you have one. It needs to be something that you do every day in order to maintain your health, happiness and sanity.

Here are some examples of self care routines:

Going to bed at a reasonable hour (10:00pm)

Waking up at an appropriate time (6:00am)

Getting enough sleep (at least 7 hours per night)

Taking care of yourself by eating right and exercising regularly (1 hour of exercise per week)

Staying away from people who bring out the worst in you (you know who they are)

I'm going to show you a list of things you can do every day that will make your life better and more enjoyable.

Here are some great guides to healthy daily routine, self respect instances, keeping true to your routine, consistency in self care:

Set Goals - have a schedule for the day

Routine - do certain things everyday, but not necessarily the same thing every day. It could be something as simple as taking a shower or brushing your teeth or doing yoga or meditation before bed, but it's good practice for habits. You should also try to do some sort of physical activity during the course of the day. This is especially important if you're working from home. If your office is close by, go there instead. If it's not, walk around outside. Get up from your desk and move around every hour or so if possible.

Eat breakfast - breakfast is important because it allows you to start off the day right with energy and focus instead of hunger which can lead to poor performance at work or school due to lack of concentration or motivation. It also helps keep blood sugar levels steady throughout the day which means you won't crash if you get too much sugar late in the evening while trying to finish tasks.

Your daily routine is also about practicing self-respect. This means not only taking care of yourself physically but mentally as well. You need time for yourself and to just relax. If you're constantly stressed out or exhausted from working late or trying to balance work and family obligations, it's not going to help anyone — least of all yourself!

I have been asked to share some of my daily routine. I am not sure if this is something that everyone should do, but I feel that it is important to share what works for me. It's a mix of things that I've learned over time and some things that have happened during my life.

The first thing I do each morning is wake up, get out of bed and brush my teeth. This is a must-do activity for me because it helps me start the day with a positive mindset. If you don't do this, then it can be very difficult to get out of bed and start the day on the right foot.

The second thing I do each morning is meditate for at least 10 minutes. This gives me time to focus on myself and think about all the things I want to accomplish during the day. Meditation also allows me to calm down and prepare myself mentally for what's going to happen that day.

After meditating, I make sure my body gets moving by doing some stretches or yoga poses while lying flat on my back or stomach with one leg raised off the ground so that blood flows back into my leg muscles after sitting all day in an office chair all day long! Then I move into another stretch where I read a few pages of the book I'm currently on and then explore the rest of the day with the mindset I created for myself that morning.

Also, you have got to maintain your decision to care for yourself and these steps shouldn't be omitted.

1. Set a daily routine.

2. Do what you love every day.

3. Keep true to your routine, even when life gets busy or you get sick/tired of it.

4. Practice self respect with everything you do; be kind to yourself, others and the planet you live on!

5. Stay consistent with how you treat yourself, even if you don't want to anymore!

We all have a daily routine and it's important to keep it consistent. The more you practice self-respect, the more you'll feel good about yourself.

Here are some tips for maintaining your daily routine:

Set aside time in the morning and evening to do the things that make you feel good.

Be consistent with what you do, even if it isn't always perfect. If you miss some days or find yourself having trouble sticking with routines, don't worry! Start again or change things up a bit until they become easier for you.

Don't be afraid to experiment with new things — it might take time but eventually they will become part of your routine too!

A daily routine is a set pattern of activities that you do on a regular basis. We all have our own personal daily routines which can vary from person to person.

Your daily routine can be as simple as getting ready in the morning, going to work and coming home in the evening, or as complicated as taking care of your children, working out and cooking dinner.

A daily routine helps you to feel more organized and in control of your life. It makes it easier for you to get up in the morning, get dressed and go out the door without having to think about what needs to be done that day.

A daily routine also gives you something to look forward to throughout each day. For example, if you wake up with an alarm clock every morning then you will feel excited when it goes off because what comes next is unpredictable!

You may find that your schedule gets busy so having a consistent schedule helps keep life running smoothly by making sure that nothing falls through the cracks or gets forgotten about completely. It also helps make sure that everything gets done on time which can save time in the long run since there are less meetings involved with fewer interruptions throughout the day!

There are many ways to maintain a daily routine, but the following tips can help you create an effective schedule for yourself.

Set a realistic goal for the day. This can be a simple task or a complex one. For example, you may want to make sure that you eat breakfast every morning or get some exercise each day. Setting goals helps keep your life on track and gives you something to look forward to.

Decide on how much time you want to spend on your daily routine. This can help determine what activities will take place during each hour of your day so that they don't overlap with one another. It's also helpful if you have enough time allotted for each activity so that it doesn't feel rushed or forced upon you.

Create an accountability partner who will encourage and support your efforts (for example, your spouse). They can help remind you when it's time to stop working so hard, which is important because it can cause burnout if not taken into account carefully beforehand.

Advantages of Self Care and Respect

In today's fast-paced world where we are expected to be on the go all day long (and often while still feeling like we haven't had enough sleep) it can be tough finding time for yourself or even getting out of bed in the morning! But if you make self-care a priority in your life then there are many benefits:

Self-care is a natural way to heal and grow. It's also a way to take care of yourself, your body, mind and spirit all at once.

You'll feel better physically - Self care helps with stress relief so that you have more energy during the day when needed. It also helps keep up good health habits like exercising regularly which will help keep weight down over time too!

You'll feel happier mentally/emotionally - When someone takes care of themselves they tend not only look better physically but also internally too! Having more energy means they're able to think clearer thoughts or even just smile more easily without being preoccupied by negative thoughts anymore :) This can impact how much stressors affect them emotionally as well because now those negative feelings aren't consuming their entire day anymore.

Self-care is a great way to take care of your body and mind, which can help you feel better.

You'll sleep better if you take time for yourself in the evenings.

Your energy levels will be higher if you get some exercise during the day and eat well at night.

Taking care of yourself makes it easier for you to lose weight because your body knows how much energy it needs from food, exercise and rest (and when).

Self-care can help you to start a healthy lifestyle.

Self-care is a great way to start a healthy lifestyle. It's important that you take care of yourself and make sure that you're taking care of your body, mind and spirit so that it will be able to get through the day-to-day tasks that come with life. You need self-care because it helps keep our bodies healthy by helping us sleep better at night or even eating better foods that are good for us!

If we don't take care of ourselves then we won't be able to feel good about ourselves which leads us down an unhealthy path towards poor health habits like smoking cigarettes or drinking alcohol every day (which can lead into other problems). Self-care habits include things like exercising regularly (whether it's yoga classes or running), getting enough sleep each night (so no more than 7 hours) eating nutritious meals five times per week with fruits/vegetables instead of fatty foods like meats etcetera.....

Taking care of yourself will boost your confidence and self esteem.

Self-care is an essential part of mental health. Taking care of yourself will help you to feel better about yourself, which in turn can boost your confidence and self esteem.

In addition to feeling more confident, it's also important for maintaining a healthy relationship with others (and the world). When we take time for ourselves—whether that means taking a walk or meditating—we're able to connect with our inner-selves in ways that allow us access new perspectives on life experiences.

Doing something nice for yourself will make you feel good about yourself - The first step to building a positive relationship with yourself is to do something nice for yourself.

Just as it's important to be kind to others, it's also important for you to treat yourself with kindness and respect. When we don't take care of ourselves, we create an environment that fosters depression and anxiety in our lives. It's easy for us not only think about how much better off someone else would be if they were doing things differently but also how much better off we could be if only these problems weren't so overwhelming.

Self-esteem - Being able to look at yourself in the mirror each day and feel good about what you see helps build confidence within your own mind; which then allows us feel more confident towards other people as well! This leads into being able to over time develop healthy relationships with family members or friends who may otherwise not understand why they feel so down all the time...

Tackling Issues that Accompany Practicing Self Care and Respect

Don't let people get to you. It's not your job to protect those around you from their own emotions and feelings.

Remember that no one can tell you how to feel or what to think when it comes to something that matters a lot to you.

Don't let people get under your skin. They're just trying to be nice and make you feel better about yourself. No matter what they say, don't take it personally and don't let it affect your mood.

When you feel like you have the right to be treated as an equal, it's time to move forward. Don't let others discourage you and keep you down.

Follow these tips to ensure that your self respect is upheld while maintaining a healthy balance between self care and respect.

1. Don't get worked up by comments that may seem rude, but don't let them affect your mood or self confidence.

2. Make sure that you are taking care of yourself first and foremost, before anyone else does anything for you.

3. Be polite in all situations and relationships, even if someone makes you feel uncomfortable or hurts your feelings in some way

It's easy to get caught up in the moment, especially when you're feeling down or just want to vent. But it's important to take a step back and ask yourself if this is something that's truly worth getting worked up about.

The temptation is to react negatively after someone says something negative about you, but this will only make it worse. It can be tempting to get angry at the person who said something negative about you, but it's better to keep your focus on yourself and what you can do next time.

This doesn't mean that you should ignore what someone says – if they're directly attacking your self-esteem or telling lies about you, then it's best not to engage with them at all. But if they're trying to encourage or motivate you into doing something positive for yourself, then there are ways of dealing with this that don't involve being defensive or getting angry over things which aren't real anyway!

These are the challenges that I have faced over the years when I started to follow a healthy lifestyle.

People discouraging comments. They may not have said it in a bad way or even mean, but they just don't understand why you do this. They feel that taking care of yourself and respecting yourself is a waste of time, because they themselves are doing fine and don't need to change anything, so why should you? This is one of the most common challenges that people face when they start following a healthier lifestyle. The truth is, they're not trying to discourage you from changing your life. They're just trying to help you realize that there are people in this world who will always tell you no matter what you do, no matter how hard you try and how much effort you put in. That's just life and there's nothing we can do about it but accept it as part of our lives now remember, we all have our own personal journey and everyone has their own reasons for following a healthier lifestyle, some people might be doing it for physical reasons while others might be doing it to boost their emotional wellbeing, some because they are sick and there are those who just realized its benefits and made it a priority.

In the case of self care, it is important to know that you have made a commitment to yourself. While this may seem counterintuitive, it is essential to maintain your sanity and continue with your goals.

If you are in need of help or advice, then look no further than this article! Here we will discuss some tips on how to deal with challenges that accompany self care and respect.

The most important thing to keep in mind when dealing with challenges is not getting worked up by other people's comments. Just remember that there are always going to be people who will say negative things about you because they don't understand what you're doing or because they feel threatened by it. These people don't matter; what matters is what YOU think about yourself and what YOU do for yourself!

It is extremely important to care for your body and mind, but it can be challenging to stay motivated.

For example, if you are a busy person who has a lot on your plate, it can be hard to prioritize self-care. If you don't feel like exercising or meditating, it's easy to let these habits slide.

The same thing goes for mental health challenges, like being anxious about a project at work or an upcoming exam. You may not feel like talking about it with friends or family, so you end up bottling up all of those emotions instead.

Sometimes we need outside help in order to overcome these challenges and find peace within ourselves. We can ask our friends and family members for advice and help us get back on track with our goals or we can seek professional treatment from a counselor or therapist if necessary.

If we want to maintain healthy relationships with others while working through these challenges, then we should always be mindful of how we communicate with others around us. It's easy for us to become frustrated when someone tells us that they don't understand why we are not doing something specific (like exercising) when they know that it's beneficial for us in general.

You've probably heard the phrase "self care" a lot lately. It's being talked about by everyone from your mom to your boss, and it seems like everyone has something new to say about it. But what does all this self-care talk mean?

It means that you're taking ownership of your life and making choices that are good for you. Self-care isn't just about taking time for yourself; it's also about setting healthy boundaries around your life, so that you can live it in a way that's best for you.

Self-care is a powerful tool to help you stay balanced, healthy, and happy. It's not easy to do sometimes — especially if you're used to putting others first — but when done right, self care can be one of the most rewarding things you do as an adult.

There are times when it's just not possible or safe to do what you really want, or when you're struggling with something and feel like you need to get out of your head.

When these situations arise, it's important to take care of yourself. The most important thing is taking steps towards self-care rather than doing nothing at all.

I've had a lot of people tell me I'm crazy for doing what I do, but I feel like it's important to keep doing it.

I feel like it's my duty as a human being to speak up about self care and respect for others.

If you want to know how I handle challenges that accompany self care and respect, just ask me. The first thing is not to get worked up by people discouraging comments.

I also uphold self respect yet nor damage my relationships with others. And if someone does disrespect/injure me or anyone else, then we go our separate ways amicably.

The best way to handle challenges is to not let them get to you.

If someone makes a negative comment about something you do, don't let them get to you. If someone says something negative about your work, don't let it bother you.

The way to deal with challenges is to learn how to deal with them when they arise. When someone says something negative about what you do, just smile and say "thank you." It's not that they didn't mean it as an insult or anything; they were just trying to help. They're trying their best, and sometimes we have to remind ourselves of that.

When someone makes a negative comment about your work or life choices, just focus on what they're doing rather than what they're saying. Think about how much time and effort went into making that project or decision and ask yourself if it was worth it in the end. If the answer is no, then change course so that it will be more beneficial in the future!

Respecting yourself by taking care of yourself is one of the greatest ways to show respect for others as well because when people respect themselves, they're more likely to respect others too! By taking care of your mental and physical health through exercise or other self-care activities, you get portrayed as someone with high self discipline and respect.

We all have challenges in life that are difficult to deal with. Whether it's a family member who's not supportive or you're struggling with a health issue, there will be times when you need to take care of yourself.

It's important to know how to handle challenges so that you don't get worked up about them and so that your relationships with others don't suffer. Here are some tips for handling challenges:

Take care of yourself first. Before taking on anything else, make sure that you're taking care of yourself physically, mentally and emotionally. You may want to spend time with the people who love you, but if they're not doing what they can do to help you, then they shouldn't expect support from you.

Ask for help when needed. Sometimes we feel like we should be able to do everything on our own, but it's actually exhausting! If something is really difficult, ask someone for help — even if it's only an hour or two each week — so that you don't feel overwhelmed and stressed out by the situation.

There will always be people who don't believe in the importance of self-care and self-respect. They will tell you that your health is more important than your looks, that your mental well-being is more important than your physical body and that it's okay to sacrifice your health for a life full of fun and adventure.

The truth is that there is no one right way to do things. There are as many ways of being happy as there are people in this world, and each person has their own way of doing things that makes them happy.

So if you want to be happy, then find out what works for you and make it happen!

You see, self respect is an important part of our lives, but it can be difficult to practice. We often find ourselves in situations where we have to make difficult decisions that involve setting boundaries and saying no. It can be hard to do this without feeling guilty or worrying about how it will affect our relationships with others.

However, it is possible to uphold relationships while practicing self-compassion and self-respect. By understanding the challenges that come with self respect, we can learn how to say no without feeling guilty and set boundaries without sacrificing our relationships with others. With the right strategies, we can learn how to prioritize ourselves while still maintaining healthy relationships with those around us. .As parents, we are always teaching our children to prioritize. We teach them that no matter how much they want (or need) something, it's important to wait for the thing they want most of all. And when it comes to self-care and personal growth, I believe prioritizing should be an essential part of our lives too. The way I see it, there are three levels of priorities:1 - This can wait until later/something more important/someone else needs me right now. 2 - This is a nice-to-have in my life; maybe later or next week. 3 - This would be a significant priority for me. I probably should not schedule this now. .4 - I really have to do this now or soon. 5 - This is a low priority task. I'll do it in the next few days - or maybe even this week if I'm not too busy…

Conclusion

I've learned a lot about myself, my body and the way I think. I have taken steps to improve my health and wellness.

I am glad that I started this journey, because it has helped me realize that I am not alone in my struggles with self-love and self-care.

I find myself feeling better when I take care of myself. It is easier to be positive when you feel great!

When you feel good about yourself, you are more likely to be positive towards others as well. This can ripple out into the world and make a difference for everyone around us!

Here are some of the things I have learned:

1. You are not alone. The world is full of people who struggle with their own self esteem and self love. You are not alone in this.

2. There is hope for you! It's never too late to start loving yourself again, and it's never too late to learn how to respect yourself more than you do now.

3. You deserve the best treatment from yourself that anyone can give to anyone else - your own good treatment, not someone else's bad treatment (which might make you feel even worse).

4. No one can give you what you need except yourself - no one else can take it away from you either, because without it, you'll always be missing something vital in your life that makes life worth living; so get started today by doing something positive for yourself every day instead of waiting until tomorrow or next week or next month or next year to start treating yourself well!

There is no way around it. You have to love yourself first before you can love others. It is easy to say that people should love themselves, but how do you do it? How do you make yourself feel better?

Here are some tips to help you feel better about yourself:

1. Love the skin that you're in - one of my favorite quotes is "don't compare yourself to others", because I think it's important not to compare ourselves to others. We are all unique and beautiful in our own way, so we shouldn't worry about others' beauty or what they have or don't have when we are looking at ourselves in the mirror everyday!

2. Take care of your body - I have learned over time that if I don't take care of my body, then my mind won't be able to concentrate on other things as well! So I try not only to exercise regularly but also eat healthy food daily, so both my mind and body are happy!

3. Be kind - this is one of the most important things on this list because it makes a huge impact on yourself and others around you! It makes us happy too because we feel good about ourselves when we do nice things and put smiles on people's faces.

A lot of people say "The biggest challenge for me is to love myself. The reason is that I am afraid of being happy because I have been taught that happiness is a curse.

I am also afraid of being successful because then I would be judged as a person who does not deserve happiness.

I am afraid of being confident because then I will be judged as arrogant, selfish and self-centered.

I am afraid of being strong because then other people will perceive me as an enemy and try to bring me down."

The truth is: nobody ever dies from having too much love. It's having the wrong kind of love that kills you!

It takes practice to build self-love but it's worth it in the long run.

It's a process, not an event

It's a journey, not a destination

It's not about being perfect, it's about being consistent

It's about being kind and compassionate to yourself

It's about being patient and forgiving

You don't have to be perfect—you just need to be consistent with your self-care practices and kind and compassionate towards yourself when you inevitably slip up (and there will be times when the temptation gets too much). You'll find that practicing self-care will help build stronger relationships with your body, mind, and heart over time because they are all part of one interconnected system that needs tending if we want things like happiness or health at its core.

In addition to being mindful about how much time you put into caring for yourself each day by eating well and exercising regularly, try making time for meditation or journaling in order for yourself in between bigger chunks of work so as not lose sight of why these practices matter!

Remember that self-care doesn't have to be something difficult. It can be as simple as taking time for yourself, putting on some nice music and giving yourself a manicure or facial. You don't have to do anything expensive or extravagant, just make sure that you are doing what makes you feel good!

Quotes from Famous Individuals

These below are 10 beautiful and inspiring quotes.

- *"Self-discipline is self-caring"* – M. Scott Peck

- *"Talk to yourself like you would to someone you love"* – Brené Brown

- *"Allow yourself to enjoy each happy moment in your life"* – Steve Maraboli

- *"The challenge is not be perfect, it is to be whole"* – Jane Fonda

- *"The time to relax is when you don't have time for it"* – Sydney J. Harris

- *" Self control is the chief element in self respect, and self respect is the chief element in courage"* – Thucydides

- *"If your compassion does not include yourself, it is incomplete"* – Jack Kornfield

- *"Knowledge will give you power, but character respect"* – Bruce Lee

- *"I cannot conceive of a greater loss than the loss of one's self respect"* – Mahatma Gandhi

- *"Respect is one of the greatest expressions of love"* – Don Miguel Ruiz

Thanks for reading this book!

www.ingramcontent.com/pod-product-compliance
Lightning Source LLC
Chambersburg PA
CBHW081830250726
48657CB00011B/3550